I0072599

Praise for *Reasons NOT to Focus on Employee Experience*

"Nick takes the topic of Employee Experience and breaks it down into a no-nonsense, commonsense approach."
— DAN COCKERELL, Disney Keynote Speaker, author, 26-Year Disney Veteran, Vice President of Magic Kingdom

"An insightful and practical guide to grow your business. A must-read for anyone in CX."
— AMANDA HROMCO, Global Customer Experience Leader

"Spot on Customer Experience analysis by Nick! It's a must have for those Customer Experience professionals looking to elevate their organizational value."
— JERRY CAMPBELL, Director of E&I Ops Consumer Services at UnitedHealthcare

"From cover to cover, I get more out of this book each time I use it. This will be one of my go-to books to gift to any CX practitioner, regardless of how new or experienced they are!"
— THERESE STEINER, CX speaker, CCXP, and co-author of *F-Notes: Facilitation for Quality*

"To focus on CX, you must first focus on EX. This book will help you do just that."
— JASON ANDERSON, Director of CX/UX & Corporate Communications at BriskHeat

REASONS
<u>NOT</u>
TO FOCUS ON
EMPLOYEE
EXPERIENCE
- A Comprehensive Guide -

NICK GLIMSDAHL

© 2021 by Nick Glimsdahl
Originally self-published in 2021

All rights reserved. No portion of this book may be reproduced, stored in a retrieval system, or transmitted in any form or by any means — electronic, mechanical, photocopy, recording, scanning, or other — except for brief quotations in critical review or articles, without written permission.

To book an event or for information about special discounts for bulk book purchases, please contact Nick Glimsdahl at nicholas@glimsdahl.com or visit www.press1fornick.com.

Manufactured in the United States of America.

To my bride, Michelle, and the A-Team.

Contents

Prologue

Most of this book will be blank because there are no legitimate reasons NOT to focus on the employee.

Each chapter will start with a list of questions you can use as conversation starters.

I invite you to use this resource not only to provoke thought, but also as a functional notebook. And I'd love to hear from you about the conversations and reactions this book ignites. Please reach out to me via press1fornick.com or email me at nicholas@glimsdahl.com.

Chapter 1

Employee Experience

"Always treat your employees exactly as you want them to treat your best customers."
—Stephen R. Covey

Questions
- What is the correlation between Customer Experience (CX) and Employee Experience (EX)?
- Should you start with EX first?
- How does EX impact retention?

Chapter 2

Customer Experience

"A brand is defined by the customer's experience. The experience is delivered by the employees."
— Shep Hyken

Questions
- What is Customer Experience?
- What does it mean to you?
- If you have a strong strategy, do you need a CX program?

Chapter 3

Digital Transformation

"The enterprise that does not innovate ages and declines, and in a period of rapid change such as the present, the decline will be fast."
— Peter Drucker

Questions
- How will your customers have input in the Digital Transformation?
- How can you prioritize Digital Transformation?
- How do you measure if the transformation was successful?

Chapter 4
Culture

"Corporate culture matters. How management chooses to treat its people impacts everything for better or worse."
—Simon Sinek

Questions
- What is the correlation between culture and CX?
- Should you align the culture with your mission, vision, and values?
- Why should it matter to organization?

Chapter 5

Marketing

"People do not buy goods and services. They buy relations, stories, and magic."
—Seth Godin

Questions
- What role does marketing play in the CX and EX?
- When and how should marketing be involved in CX?
- Should marketing be involved in the customer journey?

Chapter 6

Contact Center

"Customer Service shouldn't just be a department, it should be the entire company."
— Tony Hsieh

Questions

- How would a cloud contact center help a company focus on CX and EX?
- Should a business focus on CX, EX, and business outcomes when improving the contact center?
- What should be measured in a contact center to make sure a company focuses on the customer?

Chapter 7
Sales

"Stop selling. Start Helping."
— Zig Ziglar

Questions
- How should your organization adapt the sales process to customers' needs?
- Should a sales representative be rewarded on customer lifetime value? Why or why not?
- What is the role of sales in CX?

Chapter 8

Customer Success

"A satisfied customer is the best business strategy of all."
— Michael LeBoeuf

Questions

- When should a Customer Success (CS) team get involved?
- Should Customer Lifetime Value be a metric for Customer Success?
- What length of time should a CS team stay involved?

Chapter 9

Operations

"Never tell people how to do things. Tell them what to do and they will surprise you with their ingenuity."
— *General George S. Patton*

Questions

- How should you align Operations with Digital Transformation and CX?
- How can operations reduce friction to improve EX and CX?
- How should customer data impact decisions within Operations?

Chapter 10

Customer Lifetime Value

"I think the acquisition of consumers might be on the verge of being mapped. The battlefield is going to be retention and lifetime value."
— Gary Vaynerchuk

Questions

- What is the importance of Customer Lifetime Value (CLV)?
- Can CLV justify technology investments?
- How can a company prioritize CLV internally?

In summary, there are *no* reasons not to focus on the employee experience.

ABOUT

Nick Glimsdahl is a speaker, podcast host, contact center strategist, and writer. His mission is to bring together customer expectations, employee needs, and business objectives to create a seamless experience.

Today, Nick hosts the *Press 1 For Nick* podcast, and is the Director of Contact Center Solutions at VDS. *Press 1 For Nick* is both educational and engaging, and each episode offers listeners a dynamic blend of insightful stories, best practices, and invaluable lessons. Nick's guests – each with a unique wealth of knowledge – include leaders from a variety of backgrounds and industries.

You can reach Nick by emailing him at nicholas@glimsdahl.com, visiting press1fornick.com, or scanning the QR code below.

SCAN ME

RESOURCES

Book Recommendations

All my book recommendations can be found at
https://press1fornick.com/books/

Glossary of Terms

A Glossary of CX Terms can be found at
https://press1fornick.com/glossary-of-cx-terms/

www.ingramcontent.com/pod-product-compliance
Lightning Source LLC
Chambersburg PA
CBHW070707190326
41458CB00004B/889